AMERICAN DEMOCRACY IN ACTION

Active Citizenship

Cathleen Small

LUCENT
P R E S S

Published in 2019 by
Lucent Press, an Imprint of Greenhaven Publishing, LLC
353 3rd Avenue
Suite 255
New York, NY 10010

Produced for Lucent by Calcium Creative Ltd
Designers: Clare Webber and Simon Borrough
Picture researcher: Rachel Blount
Editors: Sarah Eason and Jennifer Sanderson

Picture credits: Cover: Shutterstock: Africa Studio (bottom), Arindambanerjee (top).
Inside: Shutterstock: Olesia Bilke: p. 38; Daisy Daisy: pp. 7, 44-45; Evan El-Amin: p. 25;
EQRoy: p. 28; Everett Historical: p. 9; Feel Good Studio: p. 12; Gil C: p. 18; David Greitzer:
p. 19; Kaspars Grinvalds: p. 14; Susan M Hal: p. 39; Inked Pixels: p. 17; Michaeljung: p. 16;
Monkey Business Images: p. 41; Alexandru Nika: p. 21; Heather A Phillips: p. 31; Pikcha: p.
37; Mark Reinstein: p. 34; Joseph Sohm: p. 24; Stock_Photo_World: p. 26; Suwit 1313: p. 8;
Peter Titmuss: p. 43; Vectorfusionart: p. 11; Vince360: pp. 32, 33; Wayhome Studio: p. 15;
Ken Wolter: p. 5; Lisa F. Young: p. 29; Leonard Zhukovsky: p. 22.

Cataloging-in-Publication Data

Names: Small, Cathleen.
Title: Active citizenship / Cathleen Small.
Description: New York : Lucent Press, 2019. | Series: American democracy in action |
Includes glossary and index.
Identifiers: ISBN 9781534563964 (pbk.) | ISBN 9781534563940 (library bound)
Subjects: LCSH: Citizenship--Juvenile literature. | Communities--Juvenile literature. | Social
change--Juvenile literature.
Classification: LCC JF801.S63 2019 | DDC 323.6'5--dc23

Printed in the United States of America

CPSIA compliance information: Batch #BS18KL: For further information,
contact Greenhaven Publishing LLC, New York, New York, at 1-844-317-7404.

Please visit our website, www.greenhavenpublishing.com.
For a free color catalog of all our high-quality books,
call toll free 1-844-317-7404 or fax 1-844-317-7405.

Contents

CHAPTER 1
What Is Citizenship?

Being a citizen of the United States of America is a life dream for many and a birthright for hundreds of millions of people. People born on United States soil are automatically granted citizenship. But the United States is also a land of immigrants, many of whom aspire to one day gain their citizenship. With citizenship comes certain rights, as well as certain responsibilities.

Rights of U.S. Citizens

According to U.S. Citizenship and Immigration Services (USCIS), U.S. citizenship by birth or by **naturalization** gives people the following rights:

- Freedom of expression
- Freedom to worship
- Right to a speedy, fair trial by a jury of one's peers
- Right to vote in elections
- Right to apply for federal employment
- Right to run for elected office
- Freedom of life, liberty, and the pursuit of happiness, as stated in the Declaration of Independence

Some of these rights may seem obvious to people born into U.S. citizenship. However, to people from other countries who do not have the right to express themselves, to worship as they choose, to have their voice heard by voting, and so on, these rights represent unimaginable freedom. For them, U.S. citizenship may be a lifelong dream.

Citizens' Responsibilities

Along with these rights come some responsibilities. According to the USCIS, the responsibilities of U.S. citizens—either by birth or by naturalization—include:

- Supporting and defending the Constitution
- Staying informed of issues affecting the community
- Participating in the democratic process and in the local community
- Respecting and obeying federal, state, and local laws
- Respecting the opinions, beliefs, and rights of others
- Paying taxes to federal, state, and local authorities on a timely basis
- Serving on a jury when called
- Defending the country when the need arises

Active citizens see these particular responsibilities as rights, and they embrace their duty to take them on.

U.S. citizens have the right to freedom of expression, which allows them to voice their opinions in public.

CHAPTER 2

Being an Active Citizen

People embrace life in two ways: passively or actively. Those who passively engage in life sit back and wait to see what comes to them. On the other hand, active people get out there and make things happen.

Passive and Active

Passive students attend school, either because they want to or because the law requires them to. These students put forth the minimum of effort to finish their courses. They do not join extracurricular activities, or become involved in their school community. Passive people may adopt a similar approach to their working life when they finish school. They may find a job and perform it because they need the paycheck. They do not necessarily put forth any extra effort to try to move up in their job, or even to go the extra mile to do their job the best they can. They show up, they put in their time, and they go home.

Active people approach life differently. Active students attend school and get involved in activities, clubs, groups, student government, or any number of other extracurricular pursuits that allow them to make the most of their school time. For example, academically minded students may make the effort to take advanced placement (AP) classes, and musically creative students may opt to join the band. In the working world, active people put forth the effort to do their job as well as possible—regardless of what that job is. People do not necessarily have to have a prominent or particularly powerful career to be actively engaged. They simply take pride in what they do, and work hard to do it as well as they can. Some put forth effort in the hope of upward mobility in their career, working toward a higher position.

The same can be said of citizenship. Some people are passive citizens, while others are active citizens. The two groups live together and generally coexist without a problem. But active citizens may be more invested in their community, since they are actively engaged.

Passive Citizens

There is nothing wrong with being a passive citizen. Passive citizenship does not imply that someone is not living a law-abiding, productive life. Passive citizens just tend to keep to their own life and do not look much outside of it. They may work, attend school, obey the law, pay their bills and taxes, own or rent a home, have a family—all of the things active citizens do, too. However, because they are not actively engaged in the greater community as a whole, they may not be as invested in their community. Or at the very least, they do not have as much of a voice in their community. Since community changes affect everyone, it can be in a person's best interests to be an active voice in their community, their state, and the nation as a whole.

Active citizens are out helping in their community, even at something as simple as volunteering for community cleanup.

Active Citizens

Active citizens accept and fulfill the rights and responsibilities of being a citizen completely and in a balanced way. They do not enjoy the rights of citizenship (such as the right to worship and the right to vote) without also upholding their responsibilities, such as obeying laws, paying taxes, and being an informed citizen.

Active citizens take part in their community, and sometimes also on a larger scale—at the state, national, or global level. There is no exact definition for what one might do to be an active citizen. One example is someone volunteering their time with people or organizations that are important to them. Another example is donating goods or services to help others, such as when a natural disaster hits and people are left homeless. Even something as simple as recycling plays an active role in global environmental health.

Becoming aware of the issues in the community and the greater world at large is the first step toward active citizenship.

Recycling may seem like a simple action, but it is just one of the many ways for people to be active citizens.

THOMAS JEFFERSON ON ACTIVE CITIZENSHIP

Active citizenship is not a new concept. Thomas Jefferson spoke about it numerous times in the late eighteenth and early nineteenth centuries. At that time, the United States was a newly independent nation, still working to establish itself as independent from England. In 1790, Jefferson said to French duchess Madame D'Auville, "A good man should take his stand where the public authority marshals him," suggesting the importance of people being willing to take a stand when necessary. Jefferson commented to Thomas Mann Randolph, Jr., a member of Congress and later the governor of Virginia, that citizens needed to be informed and have convictions. In 1800, Jefferson stated, "It behooves our citizens to be on their guard, to be firm in their principles, and full of confidence in themselves. We are able to preserve our self-government if we will but think so." And in 1803, he commented to James Monroe, "Some men are born for the public. Nature by fitting them for the service of the human race on a broad scale, has stamped them with the evidences of her destination and their duty." In other words, certain people are born to be active citizens—to take leadership on being active citizens of their community and the greater world at large.

Thomas Jefferson spoke many times about the importance of active citizenship.

Jefferson was not the only politician to promote active citizenship. Most have done so at some point, but Jefferson was an early supporter of it.

CHAPTER 3

Knowledge Is Power

The first step to becoming an active citizen is becoming informed. To be active in the community or at a state or national level, citizens need to understand what is going on in their city, state, and the nation as a whole. Citizens who want to become more informed can do so by attending local meetings and events. They can also keep up with current events in the news and other media platforms.

Being an Active Participant

One way for people to become informed is to actively participate in their community. Community can have different meanings: it could be a church community, a school community, a neighborhood community, a town community, and so on. Most people can consider themselves members of numerous communities.

There are many ways to become involved in these communities. Schools, for example, typically have parent-faculty clubs that allow parents to become involved in schoolwide issues and decision-making. Students can attend these meetings, too, or they can focus their effort in other ways, such as by running for student council. Active participants in school communities will understand more about how the school runs and why certain decisions are made.

Churches and places of worship often have strong communities. Many religious programs are run by volunteer communities. Active citizens who want to become more informed about faith-based issues can easily find ways to participate in their religious community.

People who are active participants in their community make important connections and have a place to be heard.

At a local level, as a member of a city, town, or neighborhood, there are numerous way to become involved and be active citizens. One of the most powerful ways to become an active citizen is to attend local city council meetings. These meetings are open to the public, and their **agendas** and meeting information are public record. This means that they are freely available either in hard copy or on the Internet as directed by law.

There is no doubt that city council meetings can be long and tedious, and attendees may have to sit through some topics that do not particularly interest them. However, they offer a free, open forum to listen to the issues that are of interest and concern. They also give citizens a chance to speak their mind about these issues. Speaking does not have to be done in the traditional way, either. People who want to voice their opinion but are not particularly comfortable speaking in public can instead submit their comments in writing to the City Clerk.

Council Meetings

Attendees of city council meetings can also request to add an item to the agenda. For example, in one Californian city, work was scheduled to begin on an off-leash dog park. Residents from the neighborhood surrounding the proposed park were opposed to it. They requested that the item be added to the city council meeting agenda. The item was added, and many people from the neighborhood attended the meeting to speak on the agenda item.

Generally, when members of the public show up at a city council meeting, they can request a speaker card. The card gives them the chance to speak for a designated time (usually about three minutes) on any agenda item. There is also usually a public comment time during the meeting. At that time, members of the public can speak on whatever they like.

City council meetings are a great place for aspiring active citizens to have their voices heard. They can also find out more about the things happening in their community.

Again, the speaking time is usually limited to around three minutes per person, to keep the meeting moving.

There are times when the public will not be allowed to comment at city council meetings or other public meetings. The Open Public Meetings Act states that citizens be allowed to attend council meetings, but it does not require that they be allowed to speak. However, most cities are interested in hearing the feedback of local citizens, so they generally allow time for public comment.

Other Open Meetings

In addition to city council meetings, many cities and towns have open meetings of the planning commission, public works commission, safety committee, and other similar groups. Members of the public can attend these meetings, too. On a wider scale, the state and federal governments operate through a system of commissions, boards, and committees that also hold meetings. Open meeting laws grant the public the right to attend these meetings, too. There are certainly meetings at higher levels of government that the public is not allowed to attend. However, there are many meetings that do allow the public to attend and, in many cases, allow the public to comment. The public is always welcome to submit its comments in writing to any government agency.

Never underestimate the power of the public at meetings, either. One large Silicon Valley city was looking at creating a permanent homeless encampment in a quiet residential neighborhood. The residents opposed the encampment because it would be close to an elementary school. Several hundred people showed up at the city council meeting to express their opinion that the encampment would be better located in an area not near an elementary school. After hearing from the public, the city dropped the plan and began to search for a new location for the encampment.

When attending these types of meetings, smart citizens will recognize that the most effective way to get their voices heard is to be calm, respectful, well informed, and on topic. Sometimes people think they have to make noise to be heard, but that is rarely the case in a government-meeting situation. In fact, people who get up and loudly criticize an issue without offering **constructive** solutions are often not listened to at all. Citizens who provide a calm, critical assessment of a situation, who clearly understand the factors involved in the issue, and who provide some possible solutions, very often find that their opinions are carefully considered by the government authority.

Going back to the issue of the homeless encampment in the Silicon Valley city (see page 13), the opponents who stood up and screamed, "Not in my neighborhood!" were not taken very seriously. The opponents who explained their reason for opposing the plan (too close to an elementary school) and offered a solution (for example, some mentioned a vacant parcel of land adjacent to the county fairgrounds that might provide a good alternative) found that their voices were heard and their ideas considered.

Being a Smart News Consumer

In addition to being an active participant in their communities, citizens can expand their knowledge and become more informed by following the news. This is important at a local, community, state, and national level.

News is available on many platforms. But citizens need to be careful to consult reputable news sources.

Active, informed citizens will know what is going on at every level. That does not mean they spend their entire day reading every bit of news they find, though. It simply means they keep their eye on issues that are important to them at the community, local, state, and federal levels.

Many people consume news in small bites, skimming through headlines and articles when they have a spare moment.

The number of issues at any given time is overwhelming. So, most active citizens tend to focus their participation on a couple areas that are important to them. For example, parents often become active in their children's school community and stay informed about topics related to education and school. Disabled people often focus on disability-related news and issues. Women often stay informed on women's rights issues. Members of the **LGBTQ** community generally stay up-to-date on issues that affect them.

No person is an expert in every area. However, active citizens make a point of staying informed in the areas that most affect them. They also sometimes cross over into other similar areas when the need arises. For example, there's a saying that "women's rights are **civil rights**." There's also a saying that "disability rights are civil rights." And "LGBTQ rights are civil rights." So it is not unusual for an active citizen in one community to cross over to another community that is closely related. All of these rights issues that fall under the umbrella of civil rights benefit when communities work together for the greater good, so they often do.

Weeding Out Fake News

It could probably be said that 2017 was the year of **fake news**. President Trump expressed frustration with fake news nearly every day on Twitter. The term is thrown around so often that Merriam-Webster even published an article debating whether they would be adding it to the next edition of its dictionary. Whether or not you agree with President Trump's idea of fake news, the reality is that fake news does exist. There are "news" outlets on both sides of the **political spectrum**—the far left and the far right—that do not accurately report the news. Some of them publish outright lies, and some manipulate statistics to appear to represent something they do not. Others simply choose careful wording that implies a meaning that is perhaps not entirely true. They are feeding the public information that is **biased** and sometimes outright untrue.

Fake news can seem very credible, but still be heavily biased or lacking in accurate data.

MOST CREDIBLE NEWS SOURCES

So how does one find credible news sources? The answer will vary based on whom you ask. For example, many Americans and respected members of the media cite *The New York Times* as being one of the most credible news sources today. However, according to President Trump, it is a terrible outlet of fake news. **Conservative** Americans often look to FOX News as a credible source—and President Trump largely **endorses** FOX News. However, FOX News is known for having a strong conservative bias, which could affect its credibility. NPR (National Public Radio) is thought to be a credible source. However, it has a fairly strong **liberal** bias, which could affect its credibility. AP (Associated Press) is also often considered to be a reputable source.

In 2014, the Pew Research Center did a study on the most trusted news sources in the United States, factoring in both liberal and conservative respondents. The study found that *The Wall Street Journal* was the only major media outlet trusted by both conservatives and liberals. Following close behind were the BBC (British Broadcasting Company), NPR, *ABC News*, *USA Today*, Google News, and *The Economist*. So, chances are, a story from any one of these outlets is probably credible—though it may reflect the bias of the reporter.

Active citizens look carefully at news sources to ensure they are credible, rather than believing everything they see or read.

The least-trusted sources in the United States were BuzzFeed, *The Rush Limbaugh Show*, Daily Kos, *Breitbart News Network*, and *Al Jazeera America*.

It is up to informed citizens to determine which news sources are credible and which are providing fake news. FactCheck.org provides information on how to identify fake news. It suggests:

- **Check the source of the news article:** Often simply looking it up can help the reader determine whether it is a credible source. For example, if the source website is full of questionable advertisements, that is a red flag for a fake news site.
- **Read beyond the headline:** Headlines can be complete lies. Smart citizens will actually read the story and verify that it seems credible before believing what is stated in the headline.
- **Check the author:** Authors can easily make up their credentials. But a quick Internet search can help critical readers determine whether the author is legitimate.
- **Evaluate the support:** Credible news articles always use concrete sources that can be verified by anyone who reads the article. For example, "According to the Federal Trade Commission's 2017 report on…" Readers can then look up the Federal Trade Commission's 2017 report and easily check the facts. Fake news articles will use vague statements such as, "Sources say…" They do not identify who the sources are, and there is no way for readers to verify the supposed "facts" in the article.

The New York Times is thought to be a credible source, though it does have liberal bias.

Photographs can be a source of fake news. For example, it is impossible to tell if the low water levels in this reservoir are a result of drought, or if the photograph was taken at a time of year when water levels are low.

- **Check the date:** Fake news articles sometimes recycle information from old articles. For example, when covering California's historic drought in 2015, many less-than-credible news sources used images showing reservoirs at very low levels to show the magnitude of the crisis. In reality, although California was in a record drought, the images were taken at a time of year when reservoirs are always low. They were not current images from the time when the article was written. So, the images were a misleading attempt to make the drought appear even worse than it really was.

CHAPTER 4

Have Your Voice Heard

One of the most important ways people can be active citizens is also one of the easiest ways: voting. Most citizens of voting age like to vote in the presidential election every four years, but some ignore other elections. To be an active, engaged citizen, it is important to understand the different types of elections and meetings, and how to prepare to vote in them.

Primary Elections

Each state holds primary and general elections for important positions. These can include members of Congress and the president.

In primary elections, the candidates for a particular political party are narrowed down to one main candidate that the party will then endorse for the general election. For example, there are two main parties involved in presidential elections: the Republican Party and the Democratic Party. There are also smaller parties and **independent candidates**, but the Republicans and Democrats are definitely the two dominant parties in this race. Each party usually has a number of candidates interested in running for president. In 2015, for example, the Democratic Party had 6 major candidates for president, while the Republican Party had 17.

In the 2016 primary election, Hillary Clinton was the Democratic Party's nominee for president of the United States. She beat Vermont senator Bernie Sanders. Republicans voted for

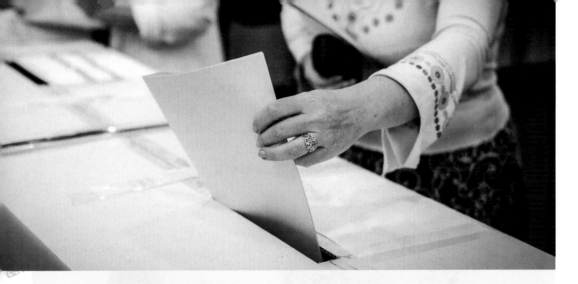

Voting is an easy way to get your voice heard. There are processes in place to help eligible voters to vote.

Donald Trump to be their nominee for president of the United States, with Trump beating Texas senator Ted Cruz for the nomination. Clinton and Trump then spent the next several months battling for the presidency. It was a very heated, **polarizing** election race, which ended with the general election in November 2016.

In presidential primaries, only citizens registered with a particular political party can vote for candidates in that party. For example, citizens registered as Democrats cannot vote in the Republican primaries—only in the Democratic primaries.

General Elections

In general elections, citizens vote to choose among candidates nominated in the primary for public office. So, in the 2016 general election, citizens voted for their choice for president. Unlike in the primaries, in the general election for president, citizens can vote for whichever candidates they wish. They can also write in candidates if they do not like any of the options.

WRITE-IN CANDIDATES

In U.S. elections, citizens can write in candidates if they do not like the options presented. However, the success of write-in candidates is quite limited. No president has ever won the general election as a write-in candidate, though some have won primary elections as write-ins. For example, in 1960, the two candidates from Massachusetts won the primary as write-ins: Richard Nixon for the Republican Party and John F. Kennedy for the Democratic Party. That same year, Kennedy won the Pennsylvania presidential primary as a write-in candidate. Other presidents who have won primaries as write-in candidates include Herbert Hoover, Franklin D. Roosevelt, and Dwight D. Eisenhower.

Citizens can write in candidates for offices other than the presidency, too. For example, Democratic senator Strom Thurmond won a seat in the U.S. Senate as a write-in candidate from South Carolina. Thurmond went on to hold that Senate seat for 48 years. At age 100, he was still serving in the Senate and is still the oldest senator in history.

There are also many examples of write-in candidates winning seats in the House of Representatives, or in state or local governments.

Citizens can write in candidates, but they should know that the write-in candidate does not have much chance of winning.

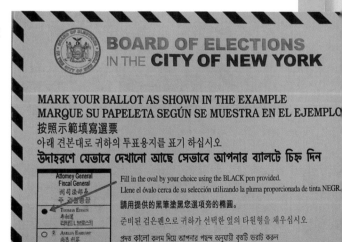

Depending on the year, general elections include the presidency and seats in the Senate, the House of Representatives, and in state and local government offices. However, they can also include **referendums**, **bond issues**, and other measures.

Often, citizens are excited to vote for the president and perhaps for other government officials. However, they do not pay as much attention to the legislative measures on the ballot during the general election. Citizens are not required to vote on everything on the ballot, either. They can simply go in, mark their choice for president (and anything else they are interested in), then leave.

However, to be a truly active citizen, people should engage themselves in the entire voting process—not just the major political positions and measures. Documentation is made available before elections that explains everything on the ballot. This information helps citizens make informed decisions about each candidate and each measure on the ballot. Some people choose to ignore that information and not vote for some of the pieces on the ballot. By ignoring that, they are not getting their voice heard as much as they could on matters that will most likely affect them and the people they love.

Electoral vs. Popular Vote

One unusual feature of U.S. presidential elections is the fact that the president and vice president are elected by **electoral vote**, not by **popular vote**. The popular vote is the direct vote of the people, and it is the standard for most elections. Citizens cast a vote, and the candidate or side with the most votes wins. However, the presidential election is different. It is determined by electoral vote. The electoral vote is cast by the **electoral college**. Each state has a number of delegates, or representatives, in the electoral college, depending on the state's population.

States are divided into districts based on the number of people. Generally, around 711,000 people make up one congressional district. A heavily populated state such as California has many congressional districts, so it has many electors (a total of 55) in the electoral college. But a sparsely populated state such as Wyoming has only 3 electors. In total, there are 538 electors representing the 50 states. That is the same number of members as there are in the House of Representatives (435), plus the Senate (100), plus electors to represent the District of Columbia (3). The electors are generally chosen at each state's political conventions. They are usually elected officials, party leaders, or people who are strongly **affiliated** with a presidential candidate.

It might seem as though a citizen's vote for president does not matter, given that the president is elected by the electoral college. That is not at all true, because the electors in the electoral college generally vote based on how the citizens in their district voted. So, for example, if citizens in a district voted in favor of the Democratic candidate, in most cases, the elector for that region would cast a vote for the Democratic candidate. However, this is not always true, as sometimes, **faithless electors** will cast a vote that differs from how the citizens in their region voted. However, this is an unusual occurrence. Most of the time, electors vote as the citizens they represent voted.

Particularly since the 2016 election, there has been heated debate about whether the electoral college should be abolished.

It is, however, possible for a candidate to win the election based on the electoral vote, even while losing the popular vote. Most recently, Donald Trump won the presidency by gaining the majority of electoral votes. However, Hillary Clinton had approximately 3 million more popular votes than he did. How is that possible? Clinton won some major states with many electors, such as California and New York, but Trump won most of the smaller states. Those smaller states had fewer electors, but when they were all added together, they were enough to beat out the larger states won by Clinton.

President Donald Trump shocked America by winning the presidency, despite losing the popular vote by 3 million votes.

Midterm Elections

Midterm elections occur in even-numbered years that are not presidential election years. So, for example, 2012, 2016, and 2020 are presidential election years, and 2014 and 2018 are midterm election years.

In midterm elections, Americans vote for the members of the House of Representatives that represent their congressional district, as well as one-third of the senators. Senators serve six-year terms, and every two years, one-third of them is up for reelection. In this way, the Senate always has two-thirds remaining senators and one-third newly elected senators who may not have held a Senate seat before.

When election time rolls around, candidate signs are everywhere. Candidates hope to secure votes, and placing signs is one way to remind voters of their name.

Special Elections

Special elections can be called at any time. They are generally called for a specific purpose, such as filling a vacant seat in an elected office. Unlike primary and general elections, they do not fall on a designated day. They can occur whenever a need arises.

Sometimes, a state governor calls a special election when a member of the House of Representatives does not fulfill their term, either by death or by resignation. Of the 50 states, 48 have held special elections for this purpose. Only Idaho and Iowa have not.

The rules are a little stricter when a seat in the Senate becomes vacant. These seats are filled by election. But in 36 states, they are simply filled when the next general election occurs. Only 14 states hold a special election to fill vacant seats in the Senate.

The Senate does not run as well with vacancies as the House does. The House has 435 members, which means a few vacant seats really do not have much impact on votes that are held in Congress. However, the Senate has only 100 members, and if a seat is vacant in one state, that state is then only represented by one senator, which is a distinct disadvantage. Also, the Senate is often very closely balanced in terms of the number of Republicans and the number of Democrats. That means votes can be very, very close. For example, when the Trump administration attempted to pass a health care bill to **repeal** the Affordable Care Act (also known as Obamacare), the Senate was controlled by Republicans, but just barely. When three Republican senators voted against the health care bill, it was enough to kill the bill. You can imagine, then, that a vacant Senate seat or two could tip an important vote.

For this reason, most—but not all—states will allow the state governor to temporarily appoint an **interim** senator.

Conventions

Political parties in each state sponsor conventions to discuss candidates, campaign strategies, and relevant issues. The big conventions are the Democratic National Convention and the Republican National Convention, which happen in presidential election years. However, parties also hold smaller state-level conventions in other years.

Citizens can usually attend these conventions. However, they can be expensive, and tickets can be hard to come by. But a dedicated, active citizen can attend.

Caucuses

Caucuses are less formal than conventions. Caucuses are meetings that generally happen at a local (city, town, or county) level, and they are held by political party. Members of a political party gather to support a particular candidate for office, or to discuss important party-specific issues. Active citizens can attend caucuses in their area.

What Active Citizens Can Do

The U.S. election system is complex and can be confusing. However, engaged, active citizens understand the different types of meetings and elections, and they participate in them as much as possible.

Caucuses can be quite informal, like this one with a handwritten sign in Hawaii.

At a local level, members of the House of Representatives will sometimes hold town-hall meetings. Citizens can attend, ask questions, and learn more about what their elected officials are doing in Washington, D.C.

Senators, too, will sometimes travel around the state and hold rallies or meetings. Citizens can attend and share their feedback about important issues.

Any person who is over the age of 18, has U.S. citizenship, and is registered to vote can have their voice heard by voting in any and all elections. If making it to the polls in person is a problem, most states have absentee ballots that citizens can mail in to cast their votes. For voters with disabilities, who may have trouble navigating public polling places, there are accessibility measures in place. These include people who can assist with filling out the ballot, accessibility ramps for physically disabled people to access the polls, and so on.

In other words, for active citizens, there are many ways to engage and have their voices heard. Voting is one step—and a very important one.

Accommodations are put in place to help voters with disabilities cast their ballots.

CHAPTER 5

Grassroots Advocacy

Traditionally, lobbying has been one way in which people work to influence their elected officials on a particular subject. Lobbyists argue for or against a particular measure or piece of legislation. They also work to see that it is passed or not passed, depending on their goal. Organizations, corporations, and **advocacy** groups hire lobbyists to work on their behalf. It can be an effective way to influence legislation, but only a small number of people do it. A similar type of effort, but one that can be done by any active citizen, is grassroots advocacy.

Grassroots Advocacy

A grassroots advocacy is an effort by ordinary people—regular citizens, not necessarily people hired for the purpose. Anyone can join a grassroots effort—stay-at-home parents, working people with day jobs, and even interested students.

Grassroots advocacy is advocacy work done by the general public. The advocacy may be organized by an official organization, but the bulk of the work is done by people volunteering their time and effort. For example, The Arc is a well-known national organization with smaller chapters in nearly all states. The Arc's mission is to support people with intellectual and **developmental disabilities**. Part of their work involves advocacy. They work to ensure that the rights of people with disabilities are considered when new legislation is passed.

Part of how they do that is by helping coordinate and support grassroots advocacy. The Arc will send out an action alert to its partners and supporters when a particular issue comes up. They include instructions for how people can work together to support The Arc's position. Interested active citizens can then act on that alert if they choose.

In 2017, the health care bill put forth by the Trump administration was an issue of great concern among the disability community. The bill included drastic cuts to Medicare—the program that provides a huge amount of financial support for services vital to the lives of people with disabilities. Disability-focused organizations such as The Arc worked together, and asked their grassroots advocates to help. They highlighted how important Medicare is to people with disabilities, and why cutting or capping Medicare would cost some people their lives.

The outpouring of grassroots advocacy efforts was massive—in part because the steps taken by grassroots advocates were easily accessible. Grassroots advocates were asked to call, email, or tweet their elected officials to share stories of how Medicare serves their family or the family of a loved one.

Grassroots advocates spoke up against the Trump administration's attempts to repeal and replace the Affordable Care Act.

They were instructed to use hashtags such as #SaveMedicare and #NoCutsNoCaps on all social media posts. This was to gain the attention of elected officials whose staff members were watching social media for these hashtags. Some even posted short videos explaining how Medicare serves their loved one.

As a result, senators and members of the House of Representatives who opposed Medicare cuts spoke publicly. They shared the stories they had been sent, and asked grassroots advocates to keep speaking up. "Your voices are being heard. Keep it up!" they encouraged. And it worked. The health care bill was defeated in the Senate, and Medicare was kept intact.

California's Senator Kamala Harris has been vocal about the importance of grassroots advocates sharing their stories to support or oppose pending legislation.

This was of great importance, because the bill should have passed the Senate. It was a Republican-backed bill, and in 2017, the Senate was controlled by Republicans. However, enough people protested the injustice of certain parts of the bill (notably, the Medicare cuts) that three Republican senators flipped and did not vote for the bill. That was enough to kill it.

This is just one example of how grassroots advocacy works, but it is an important example because it shows the power grassroots advocacy can have. Often grassroots advocacy efforts are on a smaller scale—at a local or state level. But, occasionally, a national issue gets enough attention that grassroots advocates band together across the 50 states and make their voices heard.

Sometimes grassroots advocates gather in public to be heard. But, other times, they simply reach out from the comfort of their own home, via telephone, Internet, or letter.

Getting Involved

Becoming involved in grassroots advocacy is very simple. Many advocacy organizations will allow anyone to sign up for "action alerts" that they send out when they have a task for their advocates to complete. For example, the National Down Syndrome Congress sends out action alerts to its followers whenever there is legislation that will specifically affect the Down Syndrome community. The action alerts contain specific instructions for how advocates can take action.

Any organization dedicated to promoting the well-being of the people it serves is likely to have some sort of alert program. Interested advocates can join the program to be kept informed about how they can help. The National Down Syndrome Congress and The Arc are both national organizations. They are both connected to smaller local organizations that work toward the same goal. The Arc has chapters in different states. The Down Syndrome community has local advocacy groups in many states that work with the National Down Syndrome Congress on grassroots efforts.

Many of these organizations also have active presences on social media. Interested advocates can follow them and stay informed on issues that matter to them.

No Pressure

Another important factor of grassroots advocacy is that there is no required commitment. Often, people want to help out with particular issues. However, they are reluctant to become involved because they do not have much time. Most people have school, work, and family demands that keep them quite busy. However, these are not a problem with grassroots advocacy. Active citizens can simply sign up to be notified when action is needed. If they have time when they receive an alert, they take action. If an alert comes at a time when they are busy, they simply ignore it and do not take action.

In a perfect world, people would have time to act on everything. But that is not real life, and the people who organize grassroots advocacy efforts know that. They simply encourage participants to join in when they can, in whatever way they can. No effort is too small.

Grassroots advocates strongly opposed Trump's selection of Senator Jeff Sessions as Attorney General.

ACCEPTING DEFEAT

As powerful as grassroots advocacy can be, it is not always a win. Not every situation turns out like the health care bill did, with a win for the grassroots community. This can be disappointing—sometimes even heartbreaking.

One recent example was in 2016 and early 2017, when President Trump was selecting his cabinet. Several of his **appointees** were not particularly popular choices among the general public. Two of the most controversial were Betsy DeVos who was Trump's pick for Secretary of Education, and Senator Jeff Sessions who was Trump's pick for Attorney General. Many people felt DeVos was unqualified for her position. She had no experience in the public school system, which educates a huge percentage of children in the United States. As for Jeff Sessions, in his background, there were allegations of racism and discrimination against students with disabilities.

The Senate is in charge of confirming cabinet nominees, so grassroots advocates worked to convince senators not to confirm DeVos or Sessions. Their efforts did not pay off, though. Both were confirmed—though DeVos was confirmed by the narrowest margin in history. She holds the distinction of being the first cabinet nominee to be confirmed only after the vice president stepped in to cast a tie-breaking vote.

The confirmation of both cabinet members was disappointing for grassroots advocates who worked to try to prevent it. But the advocates realized it was all part of the process. There are wins, but there are also losses. Disappointed advocates took a few days to grieve the loss, then got back up to advocate for the next issue of concern.

Active citizens who want to get involved can start by searching for opportunities online. Keying in something like "how do I get involved in grassroots advocacy" yields pages of results. Many pages are from organizations looking for grassroots advocates. Two organizations in the state of Connecticut also put together an Advocacy Toolkit for the Early Years Advocacy Groups. It was designed for people who are interested in grassroots advocacy on issues that affect children and teenagers.

At a more-focused level, though, citizens can search for a specific area of interest. For example, with a small amount of searching, someone with a loved one who has battled cancer could stumble upon the International Cancer Advocacy Network (ICAN). ICAN has a grassroots advocacy toolkit which interested advocates can download and look over.

Effective Grassroots Advocacy

The best grassroots advocates form relationships with their elected officials, share their stories, and take action when needed. Advocacy might seem to be a lot of work, but it is not. It is all about being yourself and sharing your story with people.

Forming Relationships with Officials

Forming relationships with elected officials is not as difficult or as scary as it sounds. They all have websites with links to their email, or Internet forms people can fill out when they want to voice an opinion. Both of these methods generally go to **staffers**. The elected officials receive so much mail on a daily basis that it would be impossible to keep up. That is not a bad thing. Staffers can hold the keys to the kingdom, as far as advocates are concerned.

Grassroots advocates form strong relationships with elected officials and their staffers.

Staffers specialize in particular areas, such as education, health, disability, and so on. So when a grassroots advocate sends an email or a web response about an education issue, a staffer who is very familiar with education issues in the community will read it. That staffer will, in turn, share the concern with the elected official—particularly if there are enough people who reach out on that particular topic.

Staffers can easily be reached by telephone, too. Grassroots advocates who are comfortable making phone calls can easily reach staffers in their elected official's office, or they can even drop by the local office and meet with staffers.

Just like grassroots advocates are ordinary people making a difference, so are staffers. They may not have the high profile of the official they work for, but they are the people who get things done behind the scenes, and they are surprisingly easy to form relationships with.

Sharing Stories

As grassroots advocates, people need to have a passing familiarity with the issue at hand. For example, a group of advocates are speaking out against the passage of a particular education-related piece of legislation. Those advocates first need to understand the basics of why the legislation would be harmful to a particular population. However, they do not need to be experts on every detail of the legislation. There are paid professionals who do that for a living. They analyze bills and provide feedback to elected officials on what does and does not work about each bill. Lobbyists, too, are usually experts on the legislation they are arguing for and against.

The role of grassroots advocates is different. They have to basically know the topic at hand, but mostly they are there to share their stories. As simple as it seems, stories are what can make the difference. For example, with the health care bill that died in the Senate in 2017, lobbyists and **interest groups** spent a lot of time telling members of Congress why Medicare cuts would harm millions of Americans. They did not need grassroots advocates to tell elected officials the same data and statistics they already had. What they needed was for grassroots advocates to share their personal stories.

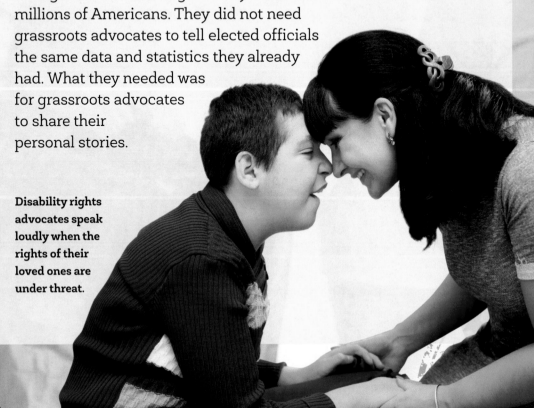

Disability rights advocates speak loudly when the rights of their loved ones are under threat.

Families of veterans participate in advocacy efforts to retain the benefits offered to military families.

People shared pictures and videos of their loved ones who would be hurt by Medicare cuts, with explanations of why. People dependent on Medicare who could speak for themselves took to social media and the press to share their stories. For those who could not speak for themselves, others shared their stories for them. Congress knew that 22 million people could end up without insurance if the health care bill passed. But seeing the faces of the people affected personalized the situation. It can be easy to ignore statistics. But it is hard to ignore the face of a child who will lose her life if her medical insurance is cut.

HOW WELL DO YOU UNDERSTAND AMERICAN DEMOCRACY?

Nearly all controversial issues will have grassroots advocates attached to them—on both sides. What are some controversial issues you can envision yourself advocating for or against?

Taking Action

Good grassroots advocates take action—when they can, and as often as they can. They do not take action on everything—they take action on the things that are most important to them. They share with others and encourage them to do the same, which further strengthens the grassroots advocacy movement.

CHAPTER 6

Volunteering

One simple and age-old way people can become active citizens is by volunteering. Volunteerism has been around for centuries. In the Colonial era, for example, colonists had to work together to survive in sometimes hostile territory. They farmed together, they worked together to build shelters, and they shared food and supplies with each other.

The First Volunteers

Formal volunteerism in America started as early as 1736, when Benjamin Franklin created the first volunteer firehouse. The concept of volunteer firefighters caught on and is still in use today. In the early nineteenth century, there was an upswing in the number of church-based volunteer organizations, which had outreach programs in a number of areas. By 1881, the American Red Cross was founded. The volunteer organization is still widely active today. And in the early twentieth century, volunteer organizations such as the Lions Club, Rotary Club, and Kiwanis were started. The Great Depression brought about the concept of volunteer-staffed soup kitchens, designed to feed the homeless, poor, and hungry. Environmental volunteerism began in the 1930s, under President Roosevelt's urging, and is still very popular today.

Children's Volunteer Opportunities

Anyone can volunteer. Some parents make it a point to take their children along with them when they do volunteer work. And youth-based organizations such as the Cub Scouts, Boy Scouts, Girl Scouts, and Daisies have a lot of volunteer projects, too.

Sometimes, it is as simple as making no-sew blankets for children in homeless shelters. Sometimes, it is spending time volunteering for a local animal shelter or charity. Other times, it is making care packages for U.S. military troops serving overseas. There are countless ways that children in organizations can volunteer.

Family Volunteer Opportunities

Sometimes families volunteer together. There are even family volunteer vacations sponsored by groups such as Discover Corps and Global Volunteers. Families can travel together and enjoy seeing a new place, while volunteering and helping the local community. One particularly popular volunteer vacation among animal-loving families is at the Best Friends Animal Sanctuary in Kanab, Utah. This is the largest no-kill animal sanctuary in the United States. There, families work together tending to the animals.

Teen Volunteer Opportunities

Older children and teens have a wealth of ways they can volunteer. Locally, there are typically volunteer opportunities at local libraries, youth centers, and animal shelters. Nursing homes and elder-care facilities often have volunteer opportunities for teens and young adults who want to work with their residents. Teens interested in working in the medical field can often volunteer at hospitals.

Volunteering at a local soup kitchen is just one way active teens can help out in their community.

School-Sponsored Volunteer Opportunities

Schools will often sponsor volunteer opportunities for teens. Sometimes, they involve traveling to another country. For those summer programs, teens travel to a poor country to help build shelters, teach children, or otherwise work to improve living conditions. Sometimes, they are one-day local opportunities, such as a town clean-up day or a car wash to raise funds for a particular charity.

CORPORATE VOLUNTEERISM

More and more corporations are beginning to offer and support volunteerism. For example, some corporations sponsor and volunteer at local nonprofit events. Other corporations participate in large-scale, targeted volunteerism. For example, pharmaceutical giant Genentech hosts a yearly Genentech Gives Back Week each June. Employees spend the week participating in local volunteer activities, such as community clean-up days, and raising money for local and international charities. Each year, employees raise hundreds of thousands of dollars for charity and serve more than a hundred nonprofit organizations. The week ends with a huge charity concert featuring three or four popular musicians, raising even more money for charity.

The Girl Scouts of America participate in a lot of volunteer activities to benefit their communities.

Alternative Volunteer Opportunities

Volunteering one's time is free and is an excellent way to be an active citizen. But what about people who simply do not have the time? In such cases, money is another way to volunteer. People in these situations may not have a lot of time to spare, but they can often spare some money to help a volunteer cause. For example, women's shelters are often in need of supplies to feed and clothe the children who come into the shelters with their mothers. Busy families who do not have a lot of time to volunteer can do their part by collecting children's clothes and dropping them off. They can even order several cases of diapers in different sizes to be delivered to the facility. All it takes is a few minutes to call an organization such as a shelter and ask what their needs are, then fulfill them. If even driving over is too much of a commitment, there's always online shopping where whatever is needed can be delivered to the organization.

In other words, to be an active citizen, no volunteer effort is too small. Every effort a person makes is one more step toward being an active citizen who engages in their community, state, nation, and the world.

Active Citizenship in Action

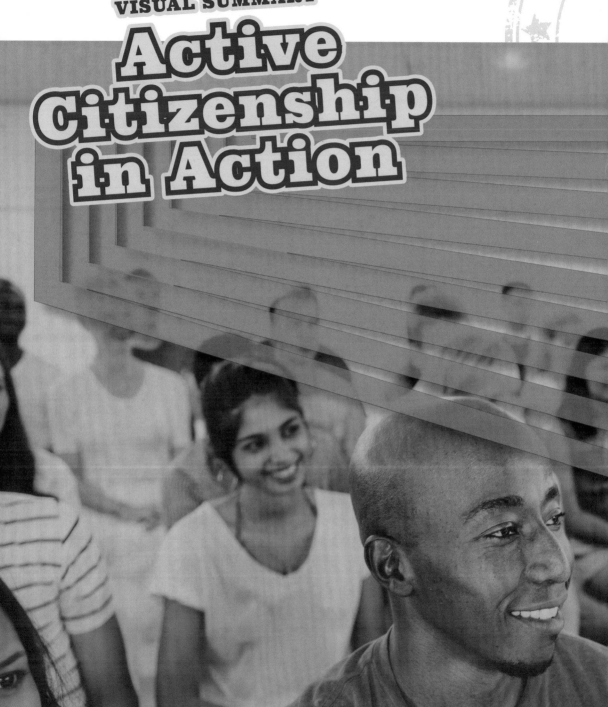

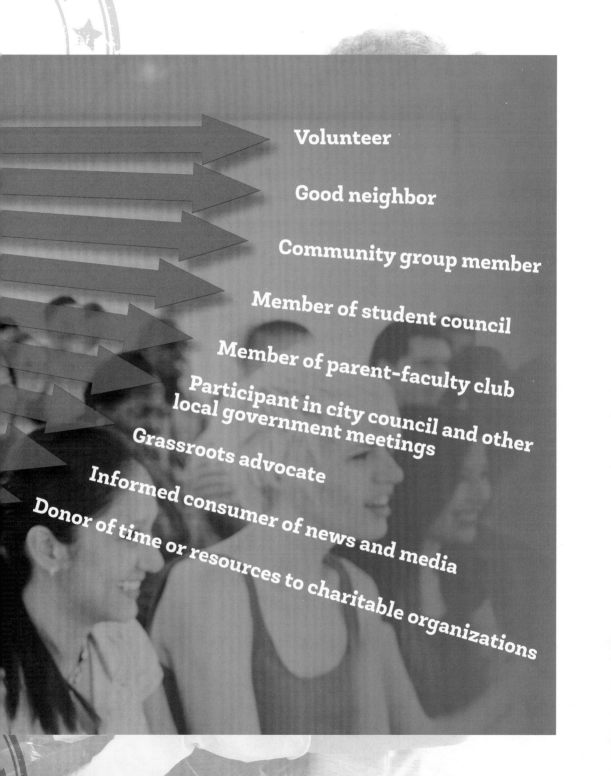

Volunteer

Good neighbor

Community group member

Member of student council

Member of parent-faculty club

Participant in city council and other local government meetings

Grassroots advocate

Informed consumer of news and media

Donor of time or resources to charitable organizations

Glossary

advocacy Public support for a specific cause.

affiliated Closely connected with a group or an organization.

agendas Lists of items to be discussed at a meeting.

appointees People to whom jobs are assigned.

biased Preferring one person, thing, or idea over another in an unfair way.

bond issues Debt instruments the government uses to raise money.

civil rights The rights of all citizens to political and social freedom and to equality.

conservative Describes one who values traditional systems and is cautious about new innovation.

constructive Positive and helpful.

developmental disabilities Chronic conditions that cause mental and/or physical impairment.

electoral college The body of official voters, representing each state, who formally cast the votes for the president of the United States.

electoral vote The vote by the electoral college.

endorses Declares support for.

faithless electors Members of the electoral college who do not vote for the candidate they had pledged to support.

fake news Misinformation and/or lies that are spread as the truth.

independent candidates Electoral candidates who are not affiliated with any particular political party.

interest groups Groups of people seeking to influence public policy based on a common belief or concern.

interim Temporary.

LGBTQ An acronym used to describe the community of people who are lesbian, gay, bisexual, transgender, queer, and other identities.

liberal One who is open to new ideas and innovation and is willing to change traditional systems.

naturalization Admittance of a foreign-born person to the citizenship of a particular country.

polarizing Dividing into two contrasting sets of beliefs or opinions.

political spectrum The range of political views from extremely conservative (far right) to extremely liberal (far left).

popular vote A simple form of election in which the candidate with the most votes wins.

referendums General votes by the electorate on single political questions.

repeal Cancel.

staffers The employees who work for a political figure.

For More Information

Books

Clinton, Chelsea. *It's Your World: Get Informed, Get Inspired & Get Going!* New York, NY: Puffin Books, 2017.

Gay, Kathlyn. *Activism* (It Happened to Me). Lanham, MD: Rowman & Littlefield, 2016.

Marcovitz, Hal. *Teens & Volunteerism*. Broomall, PA: Mason Crest, 2014.

Thompson, Laurie Ann. *Be a Changemaker: How to Start Something That Matters*. New York, NY: Simon Pulse/Beyond Words, 2014.

Websites

Habitat for Humanity offers specific youth programs in many regions:
www.habitat.org/volunteer/near-you/youth-programs

The Red Cross has a specific youth section with a wealth of information about ways youth can volunteer in their community:
www.redcrossyouth.org/scholarships/be-a-volunteer

This website allows users to search for local volunteer opportunities in areas that interest them:
www.volunteermatch.org

For teens interested in advocacy and activism, the Youth Advocacy Project is a fantastic resource, full of ideas, examples, and toolkits:
www.youthactivismproject.org

Publisher's note to educators and parents: Our editors have carefully reviewed these websites to ensure that they are suitable for students. Many websites change frequently, however, and we cannot guarantee that a site's future contents will continue to meet our high standards of quality and educational value. Be advised that students should be closely supervised whenever they access the Internet.

Index